Name

....

Allotment Number

....

Location

....

Phone Number

....

Email

....

Current Allotment
Floor Plan

Target Floor Plan

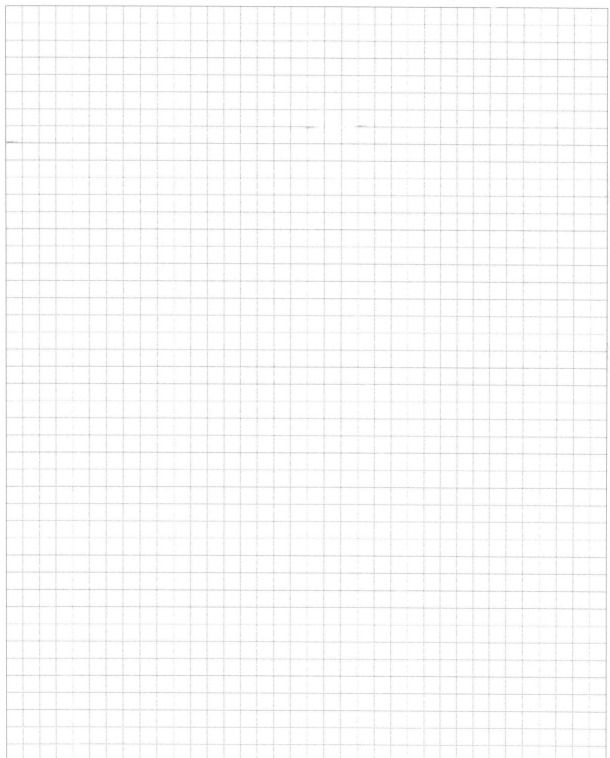

Extra sheets

Because not all plans are straight forward

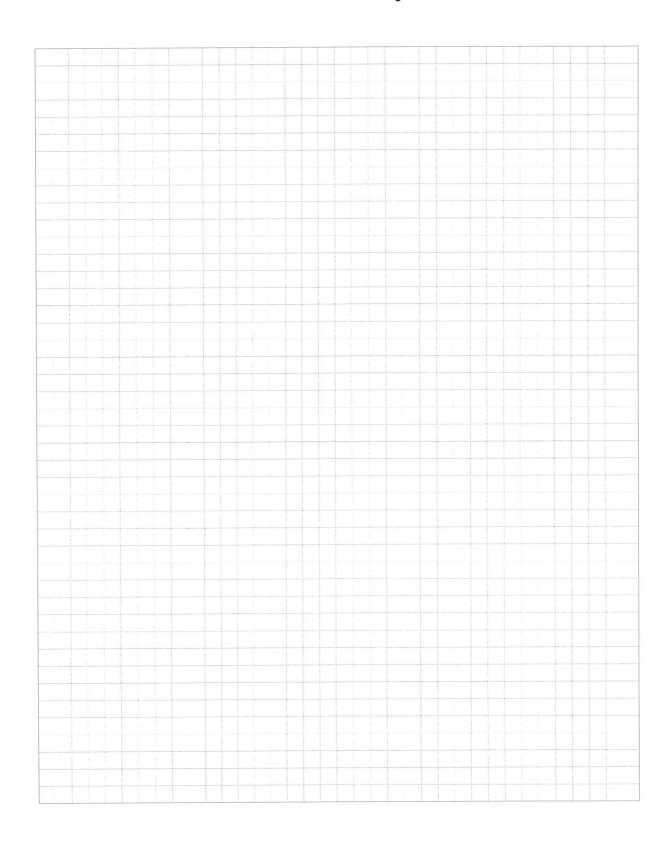

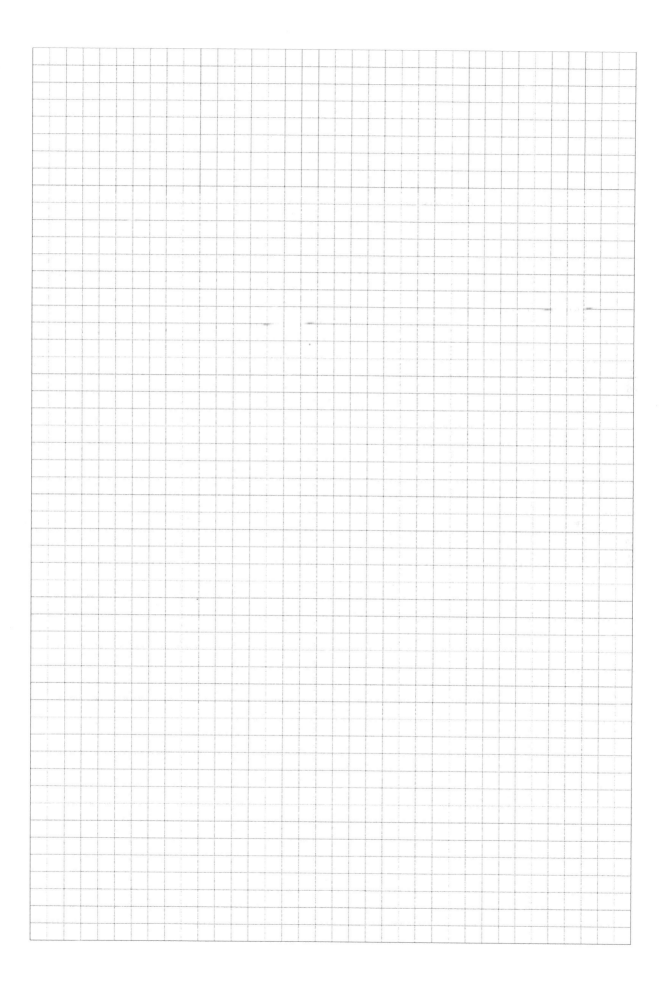

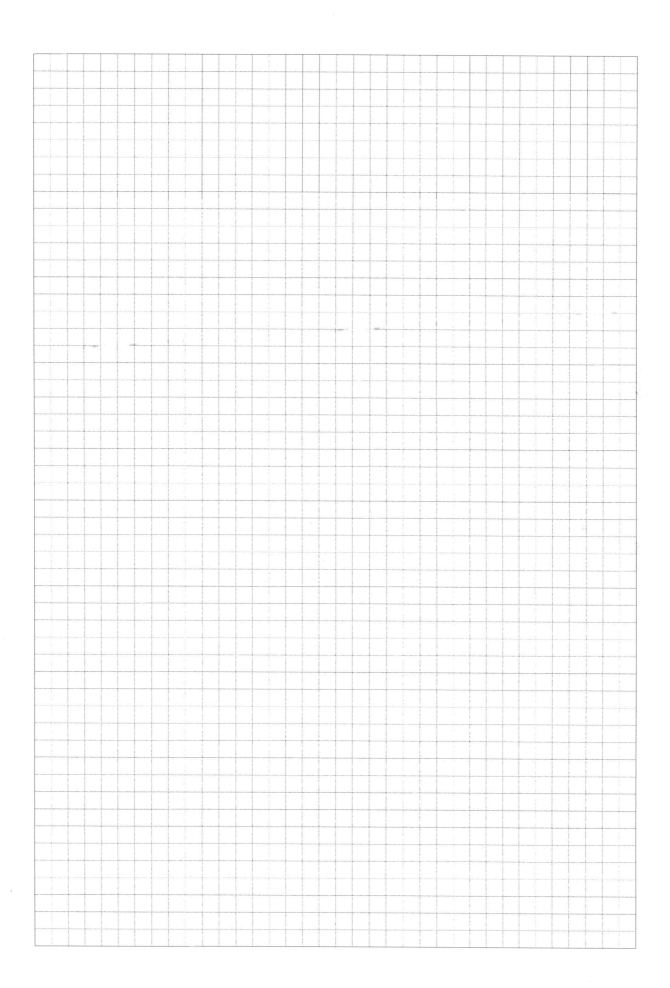

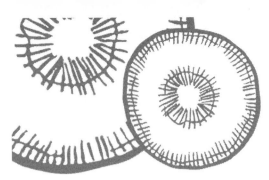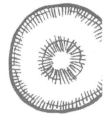

Vegetables Grown in Previous Year

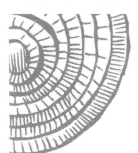

Vegetables To Grow This Year

Seeds In Collection

Seeds To Purchase

Extra Items To Get

Notes

January

Jobs To Do

Seeds To Sow

Plants To Harvest

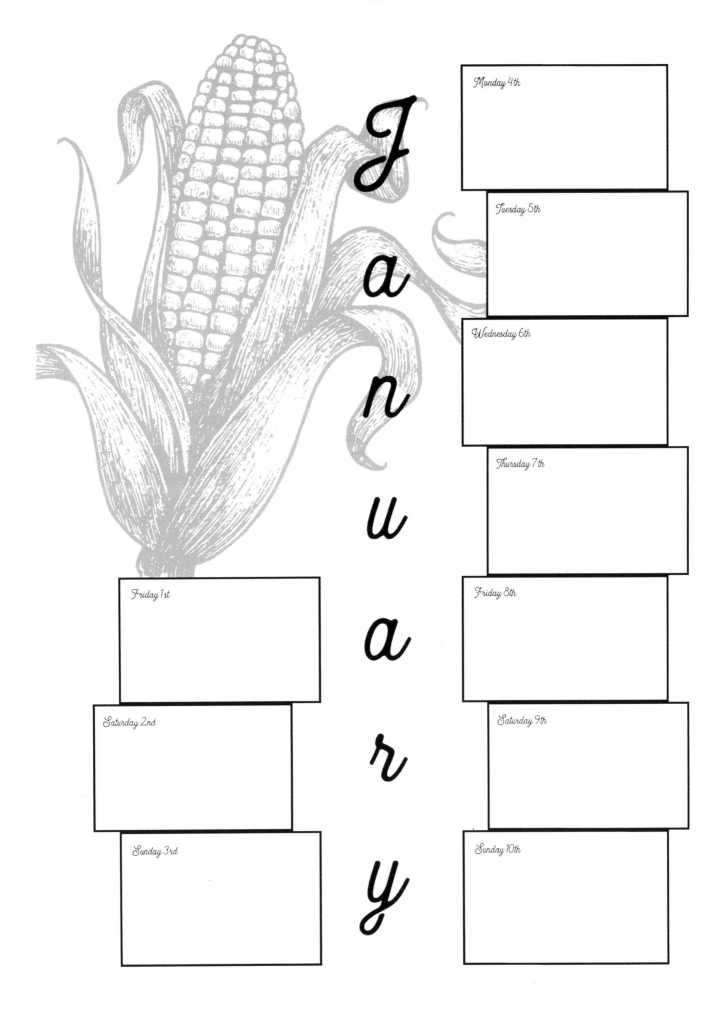

January

Monday 4th

Tuesday 5th

Wednesday 6th

Thursday 7th

Friday 8th

Saturday 9th

Sunday 10th

Friday 1st

Saturday 2nd

Sunday 3rd

Monday 11th

Monday 18th

Tuesday 12th

Tuesday 19th

Wednesday 13th

Wednesday 20th

Thursday 14th

Thursday 21st

Friday 15th

Friday 22nd

Saturday 16th

Saturday 23rd

Sunday 17th

Sunday 24th

January

Monday 25th

Tuesday 26th

Wednesday 27th

Thursday 28th

Friday 29th

Saturday 30th

Sunday 31st

January

Notes

February

Jobs To Do	Seeds To Sow	Plants To Harvest

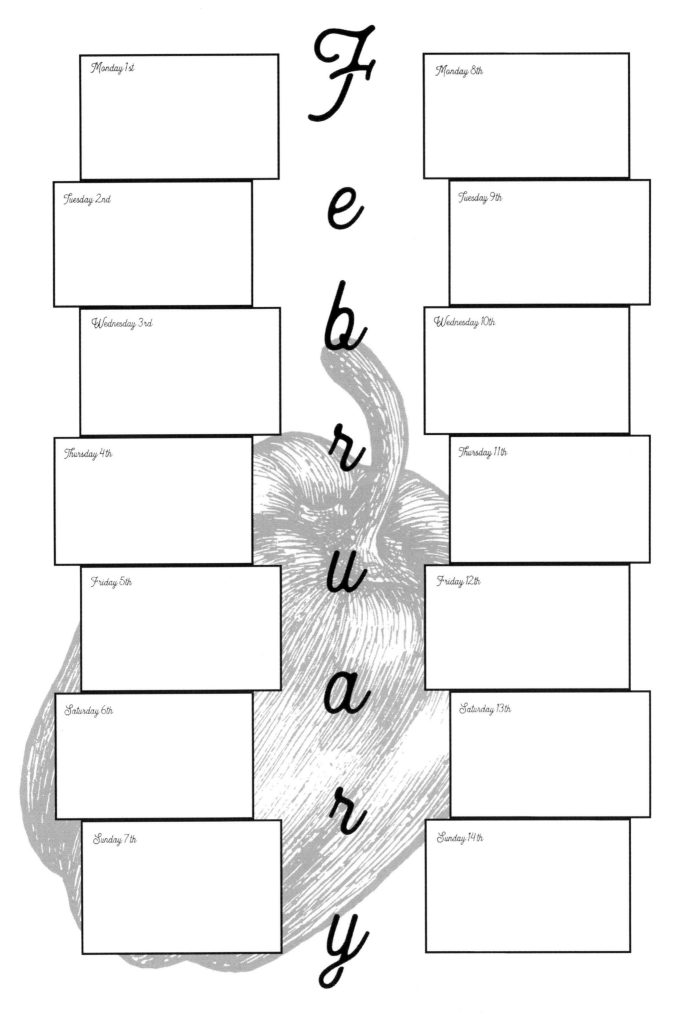

February

Monday 1st

Tuesday 2nd

Wednesday 3rd

Thursday 4th

Friday 5th

Saturday 6th

Sunday 7th

Monday 8th

Tuesday 9th

Wednesday 10th

Thursday 11th

Friday 12th

Saturday 13th

Sunday 14th

Monday 15th

Tuesday 16th

Wednesday 17th

Thursday 18th

Friday 19th

Saturday 20th

Sunday 21st

Monday 22nd

Tuesday 23rd

Wednesday 24th

Thursday 25th

Friday 26th

Saturday 27th

Sunday 28th

February

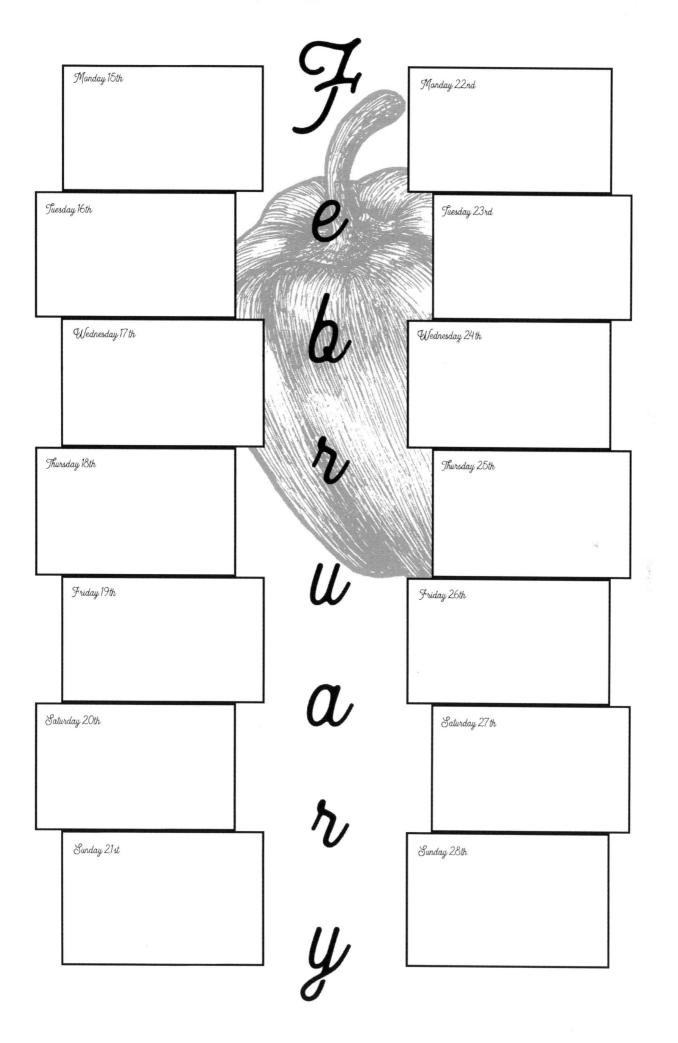

March

Jobs To Do

Seeds To Sow

Plants To Harvest

March

Monday 1st

Tuesday 2nd

Wednesday 3rd

Thursday 4th

Friday 5th

Saturday 6th

Sunday 7th

Monday 8th

Tuesday 9th

Wednesday 10th

Thursday 11th

Friday 12th

Saturday 13th

Sunday 14th

Monday 15th

Monday 22nd

Tuesday 16th

Tuesday 23rd

Wednesday 17th

Wednesday 24th

M

Thursday 18th

Thursday 25th

a

Friday 19th

Friday 26th

r

Saturday 20th

Saturday 27th

c

Sunday 21st

Sunday 28th

h

Monday 29th

Tuesday 30th

Wednesday 31st

March

Notes

Notes

April

Jobs To Do

Seeds To Sow

Plants To Harvest

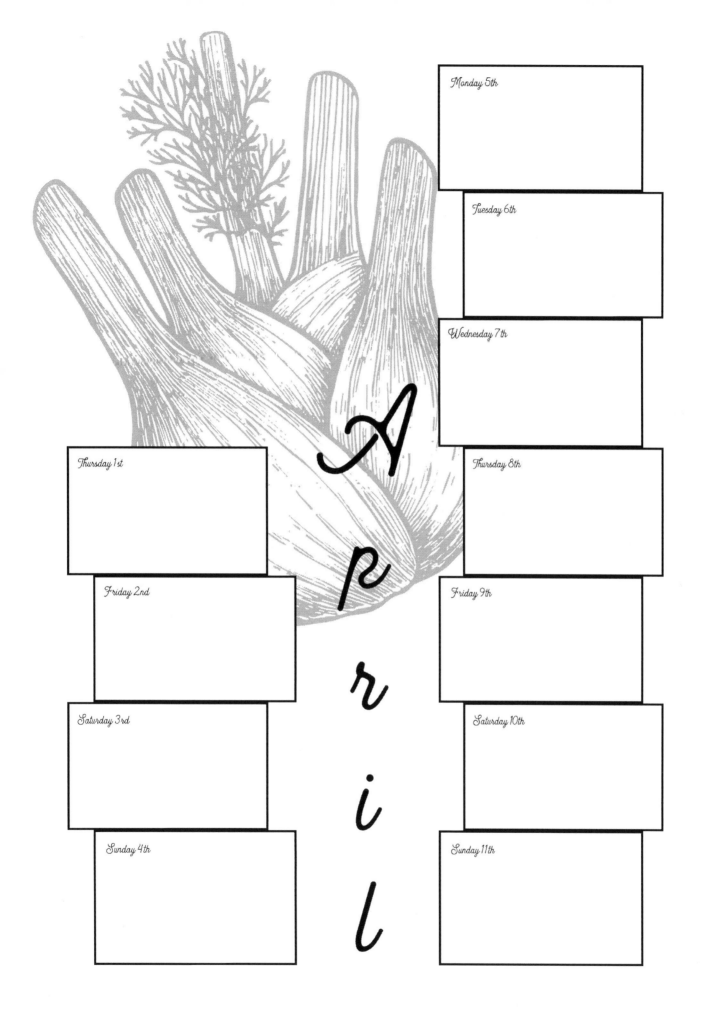

Thursday 1st

Friday 2nd

Saturday 3rd

Sunday 4th

Monday 5th

Tuesday 6th

Wednesday 7th

Thursday 8th

Friday 9th

Saturday 10th

Sunday 11th

April

Monday 12th

Monday 19th

Tuesday 13th

Tuesday 20th

Wednesday 14th

Wednesday 21st

Thursday 15th

Thursday 22nd

Friday 16th

Friday 23rd

Saturday 17th

Saturday 24th

Sunday 18th

Sunday 25th

April

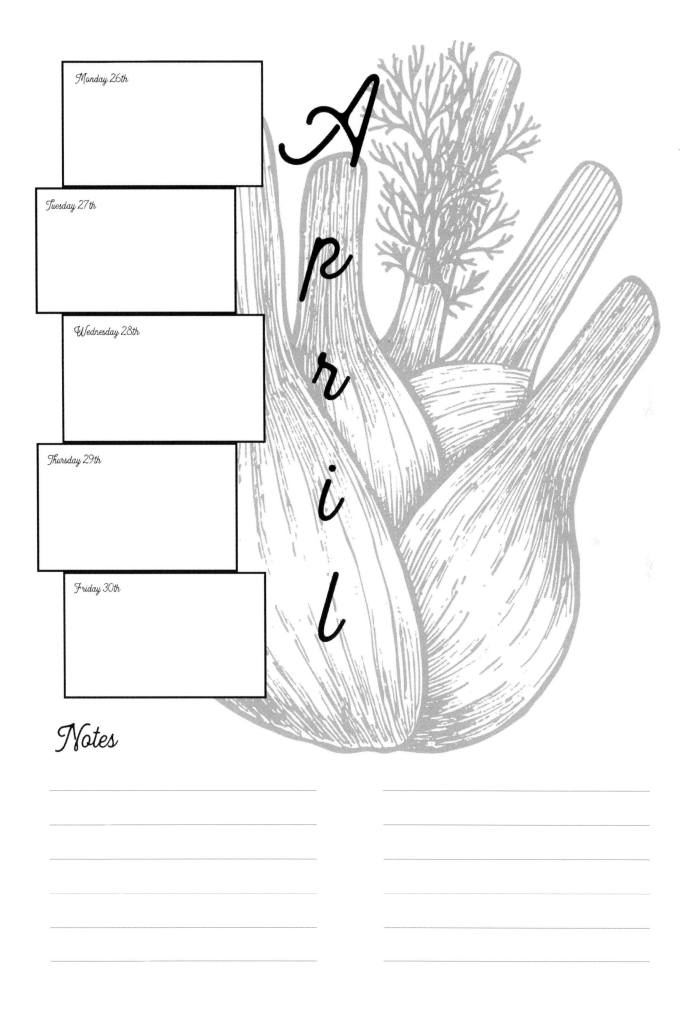

Monday 26th

Tuesday 27th

Wednesday 28th

Thursday 29th

Friday 30th

April

Notes

May

Jobs To Do	Seeds To Sow	Plants To Harvest

Monday 3rd

Tuesday 4th

Wednesday 5th

Thursday 6th

Friday 7th

Saturday 8th

Sunday 9th

Saturday 1st

Sunday 2nd

May

May

Monday 10th

Tuesday 11th

Wednesday 12th

Thursday 13th

Friday 14th

Saturday 15th

Sunday 16th

Monday 17th

Tuesday 18th

Wednesday 19th

Thursday 20th

Friday 21st

Saturday 22nd

Sunday 23rd

Monday 24th

Monday 31st

Tuesday 25th

May

Notes

Wednesday 26th

Thursday 27th

Friday 28th

Saturday 29th

Sunday 30th

June

Jobs To Do	Seeds To Sow	Plants To Harvest

Tuesday 1st

Monday 7th

Wednesday 2nd

Tuesday 8th

Thursday 3rd

Wednesday 9th

Friday 4th

Thursday 10th

Saturday 5th

Friday 11th

Sunday 6th

Saturday 12th

Sunday 13th

June

Monday 14th

Monday 21st

Tuesday 15th

Tuesday 22nd

Wednesday 16th

Wednesday 23rd

Thursday 17th

Thursday 24th

Friday 18th

Friday 25th

Saturday 19th

Saturday 26th

Sunday 20th

Sunday 27th

June

Monday 28th

Tuesday 29th

Wednesday 30th

June

Notes

July

Jobs To Do	Seeds To Sow	Plants To Harvest

Monday 5th

Tuesday 6th

Wednesday 7th

Thursday 8th

Friday 9th

Saturday 10th

Sunday 11th

Thursday 1st

Friday 2nd

Saturday 3rd

Sunday 4th

July

Monday 12th

Tuesday 13th

Wednesday 14th

Thursday 15th

Friday 16th

Saturday 17th

Sunday 18th

J u l y

Monday 19th

Tuesday 20th

Wednesday 21st

Thursday 22nd

Friday 23rd

Saturday 24th

Sunday 25th

Monday 26th

Tuesday 27th

Wednesday 28th

Thursday 29th

Friday 30th

Saturday 31st

July

Notes

August

Jobs To Do

Seeds To Sow

Plants To Harvest

August

Monday 2nd

Tuesday 3rd

Wednesday 4th

Thursday 5th

Friday 6th

Saturday 7th

Sunday 8th

Sunday 1st

August

Monday 9th

Tuesday 10th

Wednesday 11th

Thursday 12th

Friday 13th

Saturday 14th

Sunday 15th

Monday 16th

Tuesday 17th

Wednesday 18th

Thursday 19th

Friday 20th

Saturday 21st

Sunday 22nd

Monday 23rd

Tuesday 24th

Wednesday 25th

Thursday 26th

Friday 27th

Saturday 28th

Sunday 29th

A u g u s t

Monday 30th

Tuesday 31st

Notes

September

Jobs To Do	Seeds To Sow	Plants To Harvest

September

Wednesday 1st

Thursday 2nd

Friday 3rd

Saturday 4th

Sunday 5th

Monday 6th

Tuesday 7th

Wednesday 8th

Thursday 9th

Friday 10th

Saturday 11th

Sunday 12th

Monday 13th

Tuesday 14th

Wednesday 15th

Thursday 16th

Friday 17th

Saturday 18th

Sunday 19th

Monday 20th

Tuesday 21st

Wednesday 22nd

Thursday 23rd

Friday 24th

Saturday 25th

Sunday 26th

September

Monday 27th

Tuesday 28th

Wednesday 29th

Thursday 30th

September

Notes

October

Jobs To Do	Seeds To Sow	Plants To Harvest

October

Monday 4th

Tuesday 5th

Wednesday 6th

Thursday 7th

Friday 8th

Saturday 9th

Sunday 10th

Friday 1st

Saturday 2nd

Sunday 3rd

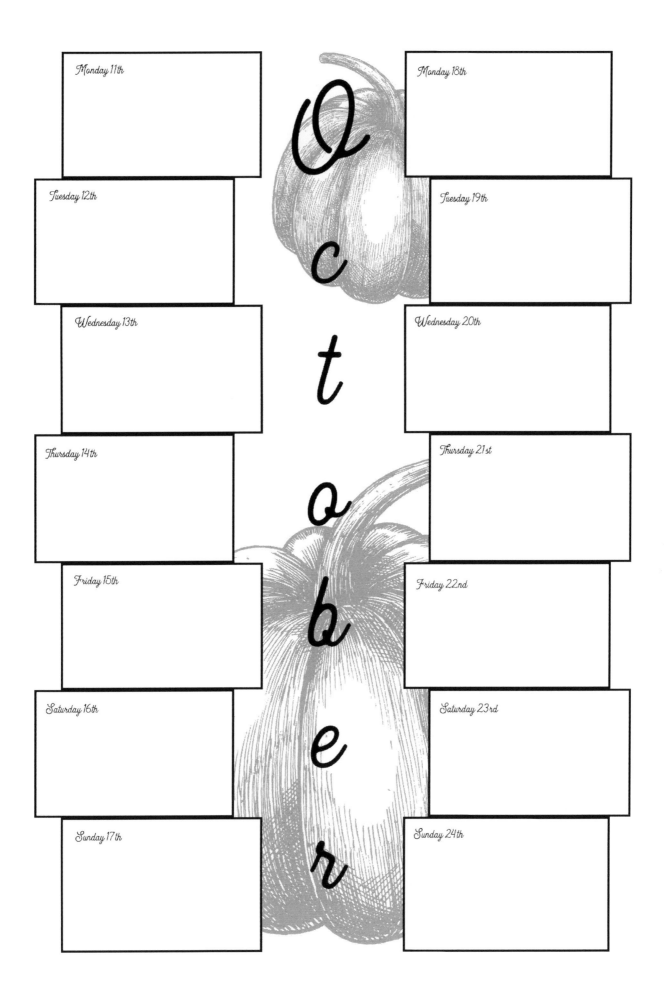

Monday 11th

Tuesday 12th

Wednesday 13th

Thursday 14th

Friday 15th

Saturday 16th

Sunday 17th

Monday 18th

Tuesday 19th

Wednesday 20th

Thursday 21st

Friday 22nd

Saturday 23rd

Sunday 24th

October

Monday 25th

Tuesday 26th

Wednesday 27th

Thursday 28th

Friday 29th

Saturday 30th

Sunday 31st

October

Notes

November

Jobs To Do	Seeds To Sow	Plants To Harvest

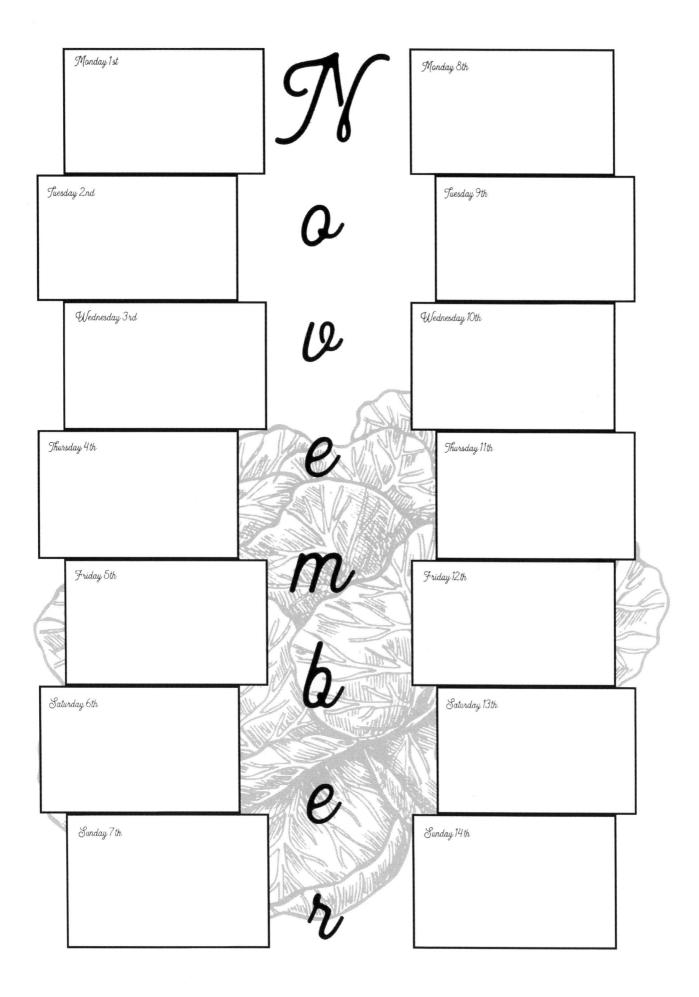

Monday 1st

Tuesday 2nd

Wednesday 3rd

Thursday 4th

Friday 5th

Saturday 6th

Sunday 7th

Monday 8th

Tuesday 9th

Wednesday 10th

Thursday 11th

Friday 12th

Saturday 13th

Sunday 14th

November

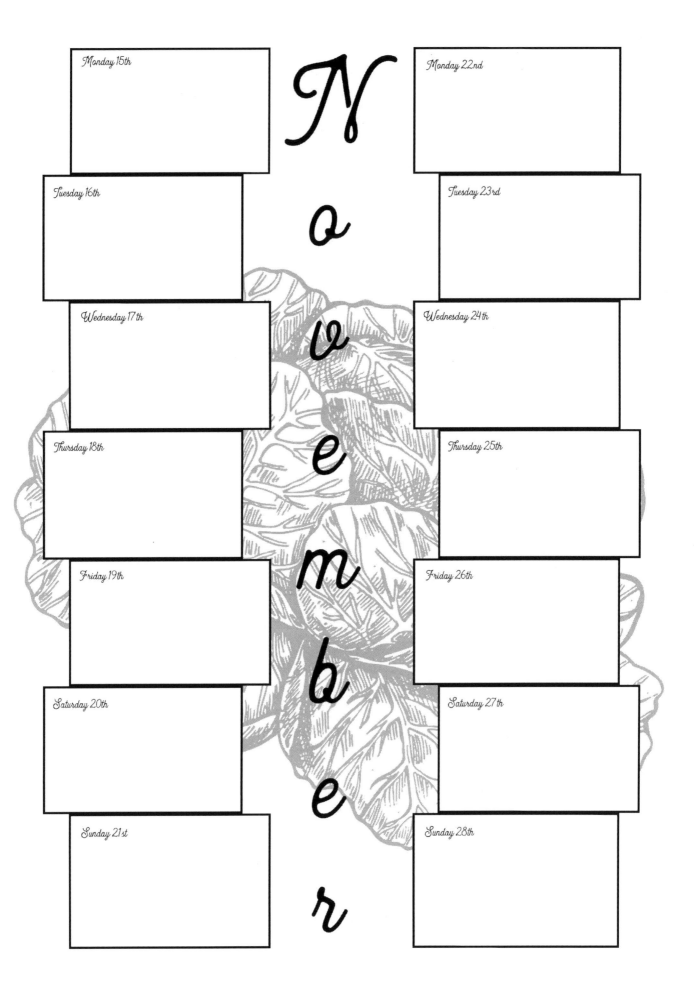

Monday 15th

Tuesday 16th

Wednesday 17th

Thursday 18th

Friday 19th

Saturday 20th

Sunday 21st

November

Monday 22nd

Tuesday 23rd

Wednesday 24th

Thursday 25th

Friday 26th

Saturday 27th

Sunday 28th

Monday 29th

Tuesday 30th

November

Notes

December

Jobs To Do	Seeds To Sow	Plants To Harvest

December

Wednesday 1st

Thursday 2nd

Friday 3rd

Saturday 4th

Sunday 5th

Monday 6th

Tuesday 7th

Wednesday 8th

Thursday 9th

Friday 10th

Saturday 11th

Sunday 12th

Monday 13th

Tuesday 14th

Wednesday 15th

Thursday 16th

Friday 17th

Saturday 18th

Sunday 19th

Monday 20th

Tuesday 21st

Wednesday 22nd

Thursday 23rd

Friday 24th

Saturday 25th

Sunday 26th

December

Monday 27th

Tuesday 28th

Wednesday 29th

Thursday 30th

Friday 31st

December

Notes

Notes

Notes

Watering & Feeding Chart

	J		F		M		A		M		J	
1												
2												
3												
4												
5												
6												
7												
8												
9												
10												
11												
12												
13												
14												
15												
16												
17												
18												
19												
20												
21												
22												
23												
24												
25												
26												
27												
28												
29												
30												
31												

Watering & Feeding Chart

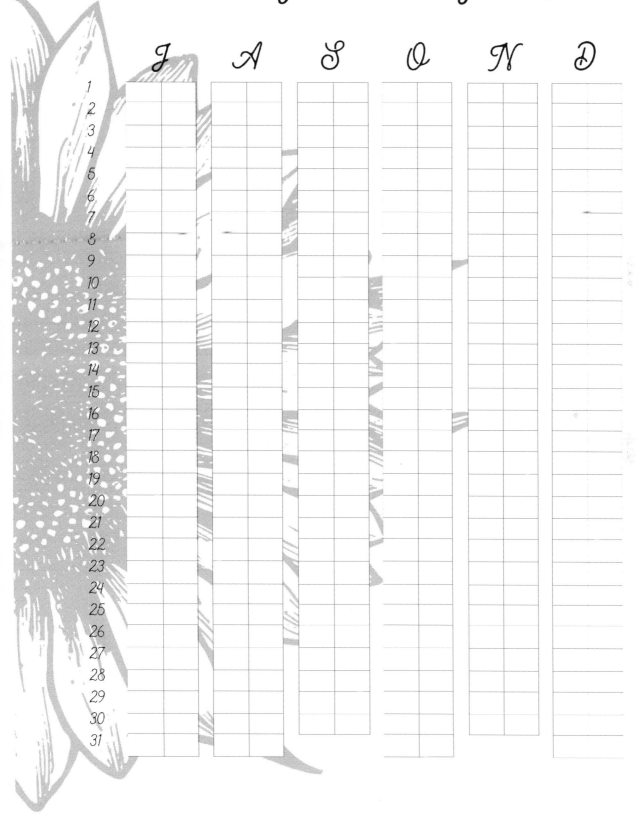

	J		A		S		O		N		D	
1												
2												
3												
4												
5												
6												
7												
8												
9												
10												
11												
12												
13												
14												
15												
16												
17												
18												
19												
20												
21												
22												
23												
24												
25												
26												
27												
28												
29												
30												
31												

Total Vegetables Harvested

Vegetable	Total Harvested

Best Weight & Size

Vegetable	Weight	Size

Recipes

Ingredients

Method

Ingredients

Method

Recipes

Ingredients

Method

Ingredients

Method

Recipes

Ingredients

Method

Ingredients

Method

Recipes

Ingredients

Method

Ingredients

Method

Recipes

Ingredients

Method

Ingredients

Method

Recipes

Ingredients

Method

Ingredients

Method

Recipes

Ingredients

Method

Ingredients

Method

Recipes

Ingredients

Method

Ingredients

Method

Printed in Great Britain
by Amazon